I Like Biographies!

Read About
Geronimo

Stephen Feinstein

Enslow Elementary
an imprint of

Enslow Publishers, Inc.

40 Industrial Road   PO Box 38
Box 398   Aldershot
Berkeley Heights, NJ 07922   Hants GU12 6BP
USA   UK

http://www.enslow.com

Words to Know

Apache (uh-PATCH-ee)—An Indian tribe that lived in what is now the southwestern United States.

Bedonkohe (bee-DON-ko-hay)—An Apache tribe that lived in what is now southern Arizona.

Chiricahua (chir-uh-CAH-wa)—Another Apache tribe in Arizona.

reservation—Land set aside by the government for a special purpose.

surrendered—Gave up.

warrior—A fighter.

wickiup (WICK-ee-up)—A round house made of tree branches and brush.

Enslow Elementary, an imprint of Enslow Publishers, Inc.

Enslow Elementary® is a registered trademark of Enslow Publishers, Inc.

Copyright © 2006 by Enslow Publishers, Inc.

All rights reserved.

No part of this book may be reproduced by any means without the written permission of the publisher.

Library of Congress Cataloging-in-Publication Data

Feinstein, Stephen.
    Read about Geronimo / Stephen Feinstein.
        p. cm. — (I like biographies!)
    Includes bibliographical references and index.
    ISBN 0-7660-2598-5
    1. Geronimo, 1829–1909—Juvenile literature. 2. Apache Indians—Kings and rulers—Biography—Juvenile literature.
3. Apache Indians—Wars—Juvenile literature. I. Title. II. Series.
    E99.A6G32422 2006
    979.004'9725'0092—dc22
    [B]
                        2005022287

Printed in the United States of America

10 9 8 7 6 5 4 3 2 1

To Our Readers: We have done our best to make sure all Internet Addresses in this book were active and appropriate when we went to press. However, the author and the publisher have no control over and assume no liability for the material available on those Internet sites or on links to other Web sites. Any comments or suggestions can be sent by e-mail to comments@enslow.com or to the address on the back cover. Every effort has been made to locate all copyright holders of material used in this book. If any errors or omissions have occurred, corrections will be made in future editions of this book.

Illustration Credits: Corel Corp., pp. 5 (photo), 17; Paul Daly, p. 15; Enslow Publishers, Inc., p. 5 (map); Fort Sill Museum, p. 22; Library of Congress, pp. 1, 7, 9, 11; National Archives, pp. 19, 21; North Wind Picture Archives, pp. 3, 13.

Cover Illustration: National Archives.

Contents

Chapter 1

Geronimo's Happy Childhood

Geronimo was born in 1823 in what is now Arizona. He belonged to a tribe called the **Bedonkohe Apache**. They lived in round houses called **wickiups**.

Their land had twisting canyons, sharp mountain peaks, and hot deserts. There were river valleys with good soil for growing crops. The Apache had lived there for more than a thousand years.

This is a photograph taken in Arizona, where Geronimo lived as a child. The map shows where the Apache lived.

COLORADO

KANSAS

ARIZONA   NEW MEXICO

OKLAHOMA

Apache

TEXAS

When Geronimo was little, his mother taught him how to take care of the crops. When he grew older, his father began teaching him the ways of an Apache **warrior**. Geronimo learned how to use a bow and arrow and a spear. By the time he was eight, Geronimo hunted rabbits and turkeys. He also learned to ride horses and run fast.

These Apache Indians were photographed in the late 1800s. They lived in wikiups like Geronimo and his family did.

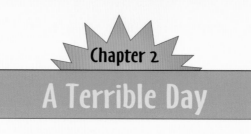
When Geronimo was seventeen, he became an Apache warrior. He married his childhood sweetheart, Alope. They had three children.

Every year, Geronimo's tribe traveled south into Mexico to trade with people. The Apache set up a camp outside the town. They traded their blankets, animal skins, and furs for knives, guns, needles, and cloth.

Apache babies slept in cradleboards. This picture of an Apache mother and baby was taken in 1903.

9

One day in 1850, Mexican soldiers attacked the Apache camp while Geronimo was in the town. The soldiers killed most of the people in the camp. Later that day, Geronimo returned to the camp. He found the bodies of his mother, his wife, and his three little children. Geronimo felt like his own life had ended.

Sometimes the Apache raided Mexican ranches. Sometimes Mexican soldiers attacked the Apache. This painting shows Geronimo with a group of stolen horses.

11

Geronimo was very angry. He said that the Mexican soldiers had to pay for what they did. The chief of the Bedonkohe Apache sent Geronimo to speak with Cochise. Cochise was chief of the **Chiricahua** Apache, another tribe.

Cochise agreed to join the fight against the Mexicans.

Geronimo and the other Apache were very angry. They got ready to fight. Here Geronimo is on horseback on the left.

13

In 1851, Geronimo led the Apache back to Mexico. There they found the soldiers near a town called Arizpe. Geronimo led the attack. When the fighting was over, the Apache had defeated the Mexican soldiers.

The Apache now looked up to Geronimo as a great warrior.

Geronimo would lead the Apache in many battles in the years to come.

15

While Geronimo was fighting the Mexicans, white settlers began moving into the Apache lands. Then the U.S. Army came to protect the settlers.

Geronimo wanted to live in peace with the settlers. But they took land from the Apache, and the soldiers shot any Apache they found. Geronimo felt that it was time to fight.

In this painting, Indians are watching a wagon train of white settlers arrive. Settlers took land away from the Apache.

Geronimo led many raids against the settlers. But more soldiers came. Life became harder for the Apache.

Many times Geronimo was captured and sent to live on a **reservation** with the rest of his people. But each time he escaped. Geronimo and his warriors hid from the soldiers in the mountains.

American soldiers captured the Apache and sent them on trains to live on reservations. In this photo, Geronimo is in the front row, third from the right.

Finally, in 1886, Geronimo knew that he could never win the fight against the settlers. He **surrendered** to General Nelson Miles of the U.S. Army. Geronimo was held prisoner in Florida, Alabama, and Oklahoma.

Geronimo died in 1909 at the reservation at Fort Sill, Oklahoma. He had fought bravely to defend his people and their way of life.

Geronimo was a brave fighter his whole life.

1823—Geronimo is born in what is now Arizona.

1841—Geronimo marries Alope.

1850—Geronimo's mother, wife, and three children are killed by Mexican soldiers.

1851—Geronimo leads an Apache attack against Mexican soldiers.

1860–1885—Geronimo battles with U.S. Army soldiers. He is captured and escapes many times.

1886—Geronimo surrenders to General Nelson Miles.

1909—Geronimo dies at the reservation at Fort Sill, Oklahoma.

Learn More

Books

Press, Petra. *The Apache.* Minneapolis: Compass Point Books, 2002.

Welch, Catherine A. *Geronimo.* Minneapolis: Lerner Publications, 2004.

Worth, Richard. *The Apache: A Proud People.* Berkeley Heights, N.J.: Enslow Publishers, Inc., 2005.

Web Sites

History Globe: Geronimo

<http://www.historyglobe.com/apache>

Click on "Anglo-Apache Conflicts," then "People," then "Geronimo."

Southwest Native Americans

<http://inkido.indiana.edu/w310work/romac/swest.htm>

Index